Mundane Emergencies

Kevin Cawley

Glass Darkly

2012

ISBN: 978-1-105-96949-2

LIONS - printed as an illustrated chapbook by P. Knittel,
Escondido, California, 1979. ELECTED SILENCE - The
Hiram Poetry Review, Fall-Winter 1982. BACKBONE - The
Lyric, 1982. WEEDS - The Lyric, 1982. HABITUATION -
The Small Pond, Winter 1982. REFRACTION - The Poet
(Mishawaka), 1982. TO AN ACTOR - The Poet
(Mishawaka), 1982. WAKA - The Poet (Mishawaka), 1982.
ERUDITION - Poetry Newsletter, Winter 1982. THE LAST
HIGHWAY ROBBER - The Villager, 1982. BATTLE OX -
The Fiddlehead, October 1982. HARD CORE ELEGANCE -
The Piedmont Literary Review, Volume VII, Issue II, 1982.
Reprinted in Fellowship of Catholic Scholars Newsletter,
Volume 16, Number 2, March 1993. NOVEMBER SNOW -
Capper's Weekly, 1983. CATSKILL - The Higginson Journal
of Poetry, 1983. CAREER ADVICE - Pendragon, Spring
1983. MAD SCIENTIST - Vassar Quarterly, Summer 1983.
REPLICATION STUDY - Blue Unicorn, June 1983. THREE
SEASONS - The Lyric, Winter 1984. HOMEMADE
BOOKMARK - The Lyric, Winter 1984. DRAGONS - Poet
Lore, Spring 1984. TUB - Blue Unicorn, October 1984.
DISTINGUISH - Poem (Huntsville), March 1985. QUEEN
OF CATS - Poem (Huntsville), March 1985. COLD - The
Little Magazine, Volume 15, Number 1, 1986. UNCOOL -
The Little Magazine, Volume 15, Number 1, 1986. Reprinted
in The Peachtree Review. TRAIN - The Laurel Review,
Winter/Summer 1987. COMMITTED - Blue Unicorn.
WALKING - Kansas Quarterly, Summer 1988. RARE
BOOKS - Fellowship of Catholic Scholars Newsletter.

TRAIN

Even the ravenous water shrew
snatching a bite to stay alive
has time to pause a moment or two.

Indentured mind, a drone of striving,
business, busyness, steams ahead --
always departing, never arriving.

Its engine might as well go dead
for all the good it does to rush
from here to here, boiler fed,

water and wood drafted to push
the void away, to cleave the air,
to bend the tendrils of clutching brush,

from here to here, never quite there,
to catch the occasional torpid cow,
sacred, not going anywhere,

to urge it off the track and now
to build up steam again, to go
as fast as natural laws allow,

leaving behind the hush, the moo,
the moment of the water shrew.

WEEDS

Tiger lily
chicory
ornamental thorn:
daffodil
mere trickery,
an early virtue born

and gone before
the weeds can yield
meek democracy --
morning-glory
lily field,
thorn and chicory.

BACKBONE

Good progress towards transparency:
my giving everyone the air
will no doubt mean the end of me.

Climbing leaves you up a tree.
Pedestrians can't find you there.
Good progress towards transparency!

What *does* a lucid eyeball see?
My retina's becoming clear
will no doubt mean the end of me.

The bare behind the barest we,
the bare beyond where bones make their
good progress towards transparency

evaporates integrity,
implies the dissolute. The bare
will no doubt mean the end of me.

Jellyfish melt in the kindly sea.
When clouds dissolve we call skies fair.
Good progress towards transparency
will no doubt mean the end of me.

DRAGONS

What dragons do amazes you.
They close their noses,
keep their fire in, acquire
quite a knack for holding back
their molten emotion.
You cannot but admire what
the magazines call quite machine-
like cool. They fool
their fellow snakes, as one mistakes
containment for control. The more
they eat their heat
the more their bellies burn and swell.
Their ears explode because the load
of acid gas
and melted gut respects no shut
no twisted lid. So let them kid
you not. The hot
internal leech inhabits each.

HOMEMADE BOOKMARK

Don't care what you say
about Vincent Millay.
By me she's OK.

Whatever you do
with the modernist crew
won't trouble me, Hugh.

Explain what you see.
But let Vincent be.
She's OK by me.

HARD CORE ELEGANCE

James Joyce, the novelist,
bragged about his minor feet,
wanted every dinner guest
to think them marvelously neat.

Samuel Beckett also wrote.
Admiring the master's wit
he forced each great foot down a boot
several sizes small for it.

He hobbled like a cripple. Corns
and blisters blossomed in his heart.
He hid behind the potted ferns.
Work in Progress! Modern Art!

THREE SEASONS

Here in the forest city
below a hill of trees
three seasons of the year the leaves
can censor what one sees.

Death has this advantage:
it opens up the view.
The time I've wasted going round
and now the stair shows through!

COMMITTED

Committed to a life
with a person called Love,
she bought herself a loom
and whistled as she wove.

Love called her his Wife
and Screwy in the Head.
He locked her in his room
and in the extra bed

committed what they used
to call Adultery.
Afterwards his Wife
confronted him, so he

declared himself Abused
and citing social norms
committed her for life
by filling out some forms.

NOVEMBER SNOW

I like a grey sky on a winter morning:
snow four inches deep and not a rabbit
making tracks, not a citizen
in sight. Without technology to warn
me, and to rouse me for that matter, habit
would have kept me guessing. But the window
proved the weatherman correct. Now lights
come on in other buildings too. My neighbors
soon emerge and try to start their cars.
I have mine half dug out already. Whiteness
makes me giddy, makes me grin -- the way
I did when I came out and saw the stars.

CAREER ADVICE

Mistake the pointing finger for the moon.
Success in criticism comes from learning
not to take the flaming fact to heart.
Describe the finger. Tell us how it rose

from flippers of the mutant fish, explain
how knuckles work, compare the nail to rhino
horn, investigate the skin. But under
no conditions look the way it points.

Otherwise you melt your eye in milk.
You lose your marbles and your better judgment
knows better than to go along with that.

Intelligent sugar stays away from tea.
Where every wave has its own bag of wind
the sea will never level with a moon.

CATSKILL

The cat's kill occurs
on account of the cat skill.
Up in the Catskill
Mountains, cats kill
exactly as elsewhere
in places less aptly
named. However
the term itself
has nothing to do
with killing: it means
cat's creek
cat's channel
cat's burn
cat's brook.
The common denominator
of this catalog
likely indicates
the cat-o'-mountain,
sometimes called
the catamount:
bobcat, wildcat,
cooncat, lynx.

ELECTED SILENCE

Stumbling among the commonplaces
Hieronymous Bosch discovered eggs
with legs. How do you do, he said.
They bowed back rather stiffly but

no words came from their cracks. He took
their inarticulate courtesy
to indicate compliance with
Economy, the country's moral code.

But in the mouth of one a message
lingered on the yellow tongue,
a slogan for a leaky yolk:
Boycott Syntax, Gradual Anarchy.

ERUDITION

I sent a painting to Monsieur Le Choc,
the prominent art critic, to get his opinion.
It had a yellow sun in the middle
surrounded by intoxicating night
with a tree in silhouette on the left-hand side.
Monsieur Le Choc corrected it with orange
house paint, enlarging the light to a cross.
I told his secretary He's
defaced it, but she only said:
Lucky he didn't fix the tree up also.
It don't look nothing like
a tree from where I sit. More like
fingers reaching for a strangle.

HABITUATION

By living in a place a while you learn
what noises you can safely disregard.
The country dog his first day in the city
keeps his ears perked up, about to startle
every time a stick-shift changes gear.
Myself no better than a dog at moving,
I had a hard time growing hard of hearing.
But in the city, to survive, you have to.
I notice the same dog lately -- nonchalant,
trotting across Main Street with a branch
clamped tightly in his teeth, like some professor
piping a smoke and pondering to work.

THE LAST HIGHWAY ROBBER

The badman beats his sword
against a thicket in the bog
and bleats for help,
quivering like the carpenter
whose silver watch he pocketed this morning:
mockery took heart
for other kinds of woodwork
and filled his skin by exploits
ineffectual where
eyes among the trees
encounter icicles along bare branches only,
no roof
no chimney breathing peat
no straw to stretch the body on inside:
where fingers
yearn to trade their stolen stones
for matches.

TO AN ACTOR

Sharpen the point.
Whittle the pencil-end.
Don't worry about making
your candle less impressive.

Light and heat
can't stand conservatism.
Money in a mattress
never sweetens dreams.

Fallow blubber
gold-brick calories
hardened arteries
no channel to the heart

tallow harbor
energy incarnate
burn your crusty water
warm the stranded poor.

REFRACTION

Crow twisted through
the pane of wrinkled glass
drinking snow
on the bend bough:
when I get up to see
the perfect plainness
of another pane
lets the bird observe me
and it flees.

TUB

The costume of philosophers
will vary from the norm.
One may wear a mackintosh
all winter (dreadful form)

another sharkskin overalls
another double-knit
another a tuxedo with
a toga under it.

Philosophers of every school
give up and join the club,
accept the normal dressing down
before they try the tub.

And all but old Diogenes
use water when they soak:
he alone prefers the fluid
medium of a joke.

BATTLE OX

At first the ox resembled other oxen.
A heavy sort of beast. We made him work
the counter at the deli serving lox
and bagels. After hours he would lurk

along the alley in the back, his horns
at ready waiting for a rumble. Gangs
of motorcycle chain-swingers torn
between scorn and admiration rang

their changes on his scarless hide.
The ox would gore them and enjoy the gore
until the old offender in him died

releasing the brighter ox within, more
placidly to snort and as he sighed
more calmly conscious minding at the store.

MAD SCIENTIST

If I could husband what I have
what breed of ox might I be getting?
Hybrid cattle armadillo
brawny, metal plated backs
on which no flies alight or vampire
bats bother to try for blood.
No openings. The predator
may advertise in vain to place
incisors in a promising
position. On the energy
that made them one by one without
parthenogenesis or sex
they carry on and only I
can slaughter them. I rather like
their animated statuary
livening up the lawn and plan
no butchery this afternoon.

REPLICATION STUDY

Food provides a measure
of the ordinary: light,
the commonest of all
the things we have in common,
implicit in the least
prepossessing meal,
in fallen fruit or hazel
nuts collected from
an untouched tree, in greens
gathered from a highway
median, in roots
of dandelion or bark
of sassafras. Light
caters every wedding,
every make-do dinner
of oatmeal cake with cheese:
the most extraordinary
snacks of candied apple
quince and plum -- as plain
as boiled potato in
their origin and their end.

LIONS

Lions mean less to us
now that we know them:
once in a dream they came
pacing from cloud cover;
even their purring could
shake up our bookkeeping.
Now they may threaten
or keep a sane distance,
come through the compound
or lounge in savannas --
bored with their mythos
we chart their behavior:
prim in our pith helmets,
wary, unwilling
to tremble in worship,
we notice how seldom
they even eat babies;
oiling our rifles
we feel almost peaceful
and sleep imperturbably,
visions of prowling
carnivorous cats
pleasing as sheep
in the mind of a Sheltie.

WAKA

A trickle
among mountains,
it receives

impressions
of the failing
maple-leaves.

They foil the flow.
They keep the stream
from leaving.

DISTINGUISH

This afternoon I wait for you. And wait.
I wander a bit. At first I speculate --
maybe you have pneumonia, maybe a cold,
wet wires or an exhausted manifold.
But pretty soon I start to take offense.
Self-pity has nothing to do with common sense.
However, in telling myself how little you care
I notice how entirely unfair
this judgment would appear to an outsider.
Suddenly my tongue comes out of hiding,
salutes my image in the window glass,
and I address myself as follows: Ass!
You'd better define your terms. Your so-called friend
has more than a friendly power to offend.

QUEEN OF CATS

Needy though not by any standard poor
the Queen of Cats requires more affection.
She takes and yells and takes and calls for more.
No courtly good will do. She craves destruction.
Solvent though not by any measure rich
her underlings supply her favorite foods.
She tries her claws out on their loving flesh
recalling the kill, a lust beyond all goods.
At large though not by any token free
local mice avoid the Queen's environs.
They guess her policy by smell and see
no reason to cooperate with tyrants.
Fit prey would show her tension at its best --
at home though not by any means at rest.

UNCOOL

Old and unimproved, I have no claim
to virtues most in vogue now: still the same
inhabitant of an unprogressive creed,
put off by novelty, put off my feed
by better fodder, chronically suspicious
of any pottage touted as delicious,
I ruminate on how to make a start --
can stodginess cause a quiver in her heart
comparable to palpitations felt
by elders when their young Susannas melt
the dignity of ages known for ice
and thaw their metaphors of paradise?
Probably not. The cool progress to cold
content to leave hot flashes to the old.

COLD

Landscape once could offer solace --
fields of snow where no one walked
seen from an upper room by night
made sorrow almost a thing to savor.

No more. The snow keeps lying there
unintended memorandum
of a better kind of grief.

All week loose windows seep and rattle.
A gallon jug in the vestibule
full of frozen anti-freeze
makes a career of standing still.

WALKING

Walking tames the wilderness
of an unfamiliar city, brings
wise correction to a strange
perspective: distance once thought great's
more accurately reckoned after
pacing it. The hill that seemed
accessible by car subsides
so any nanny goat could make it
ambling toward an uphill graze,
any human halfway fit
a fitness program on the way
to work. And once the leaves come down
those buildings lost beyond the trees
join other local furniture --
a living-room set, the conversational
cluster of a neighborhood.

THE WALK

Flame in the tree-top:
lame on the tongue
talk never touches what
walking discovers.

Leaves gone to red-orange
grieve at the frost:
words only fracture what
birds fly away from.

Ice on the ditch-water:
nice cloud of vapor
flies from the mouth as it
tries to describe it.

Crow in the tree-top
knows not to bother:
caws to the walker what
laws please a lizard.

RARE BOOKS

Laid paper laid to rest
holds up better than the best
preoccupied newsprint.
However fine the document
wood-pulp acid, culpable
convenience, leads to jaundice, illness,
yellow journalism, while
rag-heavy, out of style,
poetry survives the purge,
its alkali a desert urge
among the mills of industry,
its libertine economy
an outward range of blank space,
an inward chemistry of grace.

www.ingramcontent.com/pod-product-compliance
Lightning Source LLC
Chambersburg PA
CBHW030011040426
42337CB00012BA/731